GHOSTS AT MY

=

TOM RAWLING

Ghosts at My Back

Oxford New York

OXFORD UNIVERSITY PRESS

1982

Oxford University Press, Walton Street, Oxford OX2 6DP

London Glasgow New York Toronto
Delhi Bombay Calcutta Madras Karachi
Kuala Lumpur Singapore Hong Kong Tokyo
Nairobi Dar es Salaam Cape Town
Melbourne Auckland
and associates in
Beirut Berlin Ibadan Mexico City Nicosia

British Library Cataloguing in Publication Data
Rawling, Tom
Ghosts at my back.
I. Title
821'.914   PR.6068.A/
ISBN 0–19–211951–6

Set by King's English Typesetters Ltd
Printed in Great Britain by
J. W. Arrowsmith Ltd., Bristol

For Eva

Acknowledgements

Acknowledgements are due to the editors of the following, in
which some of the poems first appeared: *Lines Review*, Mandeville
Press Dragoncards, *New Poetry 6 Arts Council Anthology*, *Other
Poetry*, *The Anglo-Welsh Review*, *The Countryman*, *Pequod* (U.S.A.),
The Honest Ulsterman, and to Mid-Day Publications, Oxford.
11 poems are selected from 'A Sort of Killing', a booklet in the
Old Fire Station Poets Series, Mid-Day Publications (1978).

Contents

Upper Reading Room

I am wandering through Dickinson's
Dictionary of Cumberland dialect,
Nodding to old acquaintances
With whom I've never quite lost touch,
When a long-forgotten intimate,
Someone I sat next to at Infant School,
Jumps up and grabs my hand,
And I am rubbing a pace-egg
In the crease by my nose, greasing it
Till the tie-dye gorse-petal flames
Leap from an onion-skin glow;
My champion gleams, the contest begins;
The Easter Day DUNT of the blunt round ends
Of the bullet-boiled eggs, becomes
The combat rut of two Herdwick tups,
That DUNT of horns and skulls
Explodes in the Upper Reading Room.

I Am What I Was

No matter that
My firstlove declarations
Scratched in the sandstone
Parapet of Tom Butt Bridge
Are lost in lichen,
What I remember
Remains another reality.

We used to creep through coppices
Setting bow and arrow ambushes.
Chin to the ground I breathed its breath.
In the tasting of grass we were gourmets.
I roamed the fields to find
The fingertip surprise of nests,
And from a swaying tree
Watched cloud and sun pursue
Their steeplechase across the land.

Ordinary and awesome
The wind-worn hedge enduring,
Fell-sides funnelling the spate
To mark the salmon's map,
The repeated miracle of seeds,
The first cheep inside the shell,
How a raindrop can hold the sun;
My being there
Intermingled with the dale.

The Beck Insists

It's not nostalgia, I don't
Even want them to send
'The Whitehaven News' anymore,
And to set foot in the village
Is to be confused by petrol pumps
Where the smithy stood,
A loft and pigsty tarted up
As Beckside Cottage,
Unknown names on first prize tickets
Telling me that I've become
An off-comer at Ennerdale Show.

But here at home,
The beck insists on running
Through remembered alders,
A surging flow that laps the rock
Where a dipper beckons
With a white shirt bob,
Before he skims upstream
And leads me to the source.

How Hall

Enough to hear
The names of the fells –
Herdus, Pillar, and Red Pike;
Fields and flowers –
Broad Close, Wham, and Fittimer,
Gowan, ling, and cotton-grass;
Farms and their people –
How Hall, Hollins, and Howside,
Birkett, Rawling, Williamson;
Enough to know
I belonged to the place.

Imprinted

Within ten minutes
The ewe is grazing again
Calling her new-born lamb
To stiffen its hinges,
To come and ease her udder.
Already they are practising
Their recognition signals,
The particular bleat and smell,
Printing the map,
The trods to be followed.

★

They stamped me in their mould,
Made me proud of the Roman nose
They'd handed on,
The long hamstrings too
That made it natural to squat
Beside them in the garden,
Picking pods of marrowfats,
Harvesting King Edwards,
Positive that they would win
All the prizes
At the village show.

Honour thy Father and thy Mother

Word perfect in the Catechism,
I won a smile from the Inspector,
Sixpence from the teacher,
Who caned me every day to show
He had no favourites.
He was my father.
'Honour thy father and thy mother.'

He would be busy in the garden,
Yet when I went to call him
In for dinner, wasn't there,
Gone through a gap in the hedge
To the pub, the other boys told me.
By my bed I prayed
That he would 'keep his body
In temperance and soberness',
That God would help him
To master the sin.
Raised voices woke me,
But breakfast silence hid
What was wrong between them.
'Honour thy father and thy mother.'

In church, hymn-book musty
But with a smell of burning,
He was honoured as sidesman,
Read us the Lesson.
I puzzled about
How sins were visited
Upon the children.
'Honour thy father and thy mother
That thy days may be long.'
Would I die young?
The vicar bulldozed my doubts aside,
Nothing flowed from the Bishop's hands,

The bread tasted sad,
And wasn't wine strong drink?

In an argument, not a discussion,
Always an argument when he was drunk,
I said that I could love my neighbour
Without acknowledging
That Jesus was the Son of God.
With blasphemous shock
I silenced him
And went to bed.

Then in the middle of the night
He woke me, begged me
Begged me
To go in to my mother
Crying, trapped in a hairnet,
Sitting on a rumpled bed,
Rocking and keening
Gasping that I must say
I hadn't meant it,
That she could see flames
Rising round me.

On the Bible
I forswore myself,
And as she kissed me
The cock crowed.
'Succour thy father and thy mother',
Even with a lie.

Hands

Unlatch the family album,
See the old ones when they were young,
A bearded flockmaster seated,
Grandmother beside him,
Certainty in their full gaze
Of living to ninety
Surrounded by children.

Turn the pages, a corporal in puttees,
His bride in dark velvet, holding his arm,
Their eyes seem steady, seem hopeful,
But see the clenched hand at her side.

I remember the hand always tensed,
Knuckles like snow on the peaks
Hiding sharp rocks, holding back
The warmth of the Spring.

Daily her hands rubbed that special table,
So bloody special it was never used,
Spring-cleaning every season,
Wiping stains, doing penance.

I see her guarding her hands
With gloves against harsh soda,
Pushing lint under the cuticles
Where something festered.

Her hands knotted, my nails bitten
Waiting for my father, while our dinner
Dried and he drank all day
In the Conservative Club.

Fingers twisting as she made up reasons
For him, and long silences
Before the fumbled sneck, slammed door
And his harangue, boastful, moralising.

Hands happy in the garden, a sharp hoe
For weeds, canes for chrysanthemums,
Wallflowers blooming where they'd been put,
Daffodils coming up as daffodils.

Hands that could housetrain any puppy
In two weeks, teach it not to pull
Against the leash nor linger long
Sniffing at some new scent.

Hands that didn't open for my wife,
Except the index finger
Pointing out the way
She'd have dressed the babies.

Only when she nursed the stricken child
My dying father, did the hands seem free,
The first time she dared to pour a whisky
For me, thirty years too late.

Uncle

The shepherd's knife cut clean
Into the red quick
To lance the footrot pus
And rake out writhing wicks.

I needed a knife like that
To cut an arrow, notch a bow,
Make a goose-quill gun,
But my parents said
That the birthday knife
Was sharp enough,
That I might cut myself.

I showed the shepherd
The Sheffield mark,
The click of its spring.
He tested the edge on his thumb,
Then whetted both blades
Till they would shave
Hairs off the back of his hand,
And quietly said,
'Sharp knives don't slip,
But it will do
What you
Make it do,
Remember.'

Oh, the power I handled,
The blazing of trails,
The felling and shaping
Of bull-tree and kesh
Into guns.
Oh, the magic, white magic
Of peeling a Jacob wand,

The new-made sweetness
Of a sycamore sap-whistle.
Oh, what he gave
When he offered
The risk of the knife.

Johnny

A need much greater than I knew
Drew me to Croasdale Beck,
Running after Johnny's heels
To carry his trout on a twig.
To follow, to follow,
To have my boots flecked
With the buttercup gold
That he scattered,
Was all that I looked for,
The touch of his rod
Made me his squire for ever.

*

A drop of rain came through,
Hissed its hot spit on the Tortoise stove
Beside his shoemaker's bench,
While he sewed the upper to the sole
Of Bill's left boot – allowing for that corn –
And I lashed hooks to gut, practised
His whip finish till it was right,
Both of us tying knots
That didn't slip.

When we Moved

1. Whitehaven

By the sea
Women gleaning coal,
Decaying Georgian streets,
Men on the dole
Mufflered, with whippets,
The Grammar School I entered –
Someone else's territory.

2. Haig Pit

Clogs clicking,
The morning shift often woke me,
But under the streetlights
This was a stampede,
Men without jackets,
Women in shawls clutching children,
Clogs clattering,
Hooters blaring
'Haig Pit's blown up'.

3. Number 13 Inkerman Terrace

Behind our bright brass knocker
And white-lined steps,
A fire-damp of shame
Seeped from room
To curtained room,
Every minute
The risk of explosion.
I feared it, wanted it,
Feared myself for thinking it.

Bridge End

'There's always a bed for you, Tom,
Whenever you come to Bridge End',
Offered, if not an end, at least
A break in home hostilities,
A bridge of refuge, back to Ennerdale,
Hills to look up to,
Clear waters flowing.

Parents would not forbid a visit
To grandparents, and Aunt Jane
Who must have known,
But spoke of the fishing
I'd come for, in the beck
By the bridge at the end of her garden.

'Dinner at twelve', and 'Back before dark',
Were freely construed,
She found me tins and thread and such
From all the store she kept
To come in useful,
A rag I've wrapped a reel in
For fifty years.

She did not ask me
Where I'd been; I told her.
Wet feet were not a crime.
She praised my catch, however small,
Before she fed me.
I slept deep in feathers,
Woke revived by the steady tick
Of her longcase clock.

Clipping Day

Now, I remember the fear,
The ewe's flesh flinching
As shears neared her throat
For the first cut into the rise
Where new wool pushes off its past
In order to repeat it.

Then, I saw no shadow
While I orbited the sun,
My grandfather, who taught me
Exactly where to draw his smit mark,
'Two strokes across t' shoulders
And a pop at t' tailhead'.

All day identity was bleating
As I bundled fleeces,
Old outer enclosing inner new,
And kept my tally of the harvest
Stored in the dark loft.

On clipping day Grandfather surveyed us all,
His flock of sheep and men,
New growing under, out of old,
Predetermined shaped and wrapped
In the fleece of his mind.
He printed me with his family mark,
Proud passport in that country,
Not granted to off-comers.

I listened to uncles clipping and snipping,
Talking and turning the cycle of seasons,
The story of mating, lineage, and lineaments,
Hollins flock and Rawling yeomen;
The past teased out and meshed with new,
Making me one of the men.

At night I was reluctant
To wash off the grease of the day.
My mother smoothed soft blankets
For my masculine dreams.

The fleece was safe,
It turned the rain,
Slowly began to suffocate me.
I tore it from my throat
With radical words,
Went no more to clipping day,
Went South.

But wool clings,
I could not cast what lay behind,
Strands still holding me to visits
When wife and children met appraising eyes
That whistled up guilt to gather us in,
Tried to fold us again in the fold.

Two generations had to die
Before I could part with my blanket,
Sleep free with my wife
Under our own duvet.

A Sort of Killing

There had to be a killing
Of the guards
To get away
From their protective custody,
To find myself
In another country.

Though now I resurrect them,
I can see their fence
Was chain-linked to a past
That penned them too
In an inbred dale
Between clouded crags.

If we could talk now
As we should have talked then,
Would they plead visited sins
And stronger guards,
And would they claim
That drowning drink and migraine

Were unregarded cries for help?
I think I understand,
But even now
There has to be
A sort of killing
To stay free.

In the Garden

Photographs don't move,
Nobody rises from there,

But the garden line he left,
Unwinding in my hands
Brings his touch to supervise;

Steel smoothness of secateurs
Pruning hard to old wood,
Carries her approving smile.

I still plant peas in his domino five,
Cut off deadheads as she did,
And propagate the pinks they grew.

In the ordered garden,
Ghosts at my back.

Canada Goose

I am sidling through rushes,
Scanning the sliding stream
For the ring-rise of a trout,
When a hiss – not a snake, surely? –
Freezes me, foot raised,
And there at my knee
The shoe-button eye
Is staring me out.

In stiff profile, black head
White-cheeked, wooden as a duck decoy,
She sits close on the heaped mound
Plucked from her own breast,
All thought of flight forbidden
By her demanding eggs.

Birkby

Where the trunk thickens
I touch growth scars,
Above, the bands we peeled
For our Red Indian pictograms,
Clear smoother skin,
A young-leaf fountain
Streaming in the wind.

Birkby. Its name tells
The tale of birches
Here, then.

In the bark touch
Of the silver birk,
There's the thrust
Of roots through
Thin self-compost
And gravel watermark.
Fingers reach deep
To bedrock.

Fisherman to Salmon

Audacious your odyssey,
Salmo the Leaper;

You were so near your redd,
Your shrunken gut
Forbade all feeding,
Urged you to ripen;

But you came to my lure,
Betrayed yourself
For a feather.

Sea-Trout Run

With the fixed intent
Of a stalking cat,
I belly-slide to spy
Where rippled water twists
And blurs the greystone depths,
When a stray windshift opens
A moment's tunnel for slit eyes;
And then a heliograph
Is flashing; two, another, more
Sea-trout tails are fanning,
Uncertain of their station
In this flotilla come to harbour.

They have come back again,
Slipped in on last night's tide
Past Windscale towers,
Heralding that seasons still succeed,
At least, this year.

A feast lies here to be won
By stratagems of rod and line
Under the camouflage of night.
Now, in the sun
The eye tries to etch
Maps of range and aiming point
Bright enough to read
When dark deceives.

Back from the bank I notice
Earth's greenness on my palm,
And where a bramble thorn
Has clawed its line of blood.

Crossing to Fish

Above the mark of the highest tide,
Where mud and marsh become hard rock
Clean grass on gravel,
The first ford up the dale
Made itself for men to find.

Safe crossing now for swinging udders,
Tractors bouncing under bales of hay –
Sometime, a killing ground.

The Prince's men no longer bonny,
Harried in this narrow valley;
Blood oozing in the stream.

Harness-jingling Muncaster lords,
Cold-eyed, falcon-wristed;
Hoof-spray chasing Norman game.

Roman helmets out from Hardknott
Send scouts forward, interlock their shields
Against an ambush here.

Wild men come round Raven Crag,
Wade, splash, and stab,
Drive salmon to the reddening shore.

The swing-bridge creaks beside the ford
Worn boards beneath my feet,
A swaying path not air not ground;
And in the wavering dusk
Old water voices lift and fall.

Night Fisherman

I come at dusk to the dub
Where sea-trout rest,
Let the day slide behind the ridge,
Wait by the dry-stone wall
Till the distant bank advances.

I hear an old ewe's husky cough,
The water slopping slapping,
But listen, taut
For the important interjection
Of a lunging fish.

Lips taste the mist of falling dew;
The tang of trodden nettles
Cuts through the milkiness of cows;
Earth's body-scent floods in.

Skin opens to the night,
Unlocks another sense
First recognized in youth,
Found then from further back,
Before books,
Before words.

The body pulses
With the valley's beat,
Absorbing and absorbed,
Moves when the moment comes.

Boots remember boulders,
Where to turn
Half-left, then right,
A steep step down,
A trodden path,
The ancient track.

Now touch is master, blindman fingering
Of reel and rod, the hook's keen point;
Feet shuffle-feel the ground,
Delicately crunch the gravel;
Body poised ready to reach
Beneath the mirror of the pool;
Hands in time with the flexing
Spring of built bamboo,
The back-cast pulling
Storing power
For the forward drive,
The lure's leap.

Only the Body

Long after midnight,
Only the body pouring
Into the water world
Through the rod through the line
Through the searching lure,
Conjuring a trick
For sea-trout eyes.

The stars are cold and clear,
The ruse transparent.

I wade in deeper,
Share with the fish
Its lateral line
The current's push;
My fingers fifteen yards away,
Coaxing feathers
To flicker and sway.

A breath touches my cheek,
Grows to a breeze
Ruffles the pool,
Brings a drift of cloud.
The lure comes alive.

A soft pluck;
Then the barbed point
Bites deep,
Holds fast in gristle.

Through the hook through the line
Through the rod's kick
In my palm,
Only the body throbbing.

Wild Harvest

No blood on the lure
When I dressed it,
Barred teal and blue hackle
Masking the wide-gape hook.

Now in the dark pool
Panic races, twangs the line
Screeches the reel, runs
Till the rod's spring compels
Obedient circles,
Flank-flash drowning in air,
Drawn to the net
Where my loaded club
Kills.

As the torch admires
A dead eye clouds,
Yet stares its question.

Out of the shadows
Hunter ghosts come close
To weigh the wild harvest.

I wade again
Thigh-deep
In clear water.

Angler

The alder tree holds
Sea-trout at its roots,
But bars the air where
My line must unloop itself.

Merely to be here
Is to interfere;
To clear a gap
For my lure's pitch
Changes the picture
Becoming part of it.
I leave shade enough,
A minimal scar.

Blackthorn and bramble
Will scrape my back
As I edge in the dark
To the opposite shore,
Consider space and angles,
Where I stand
Anent the wild fish
And the tree.

Gone

At morning waking
There was a faint awareness,
A whiff of tallow cooling,
Gone, of no consequence,
Long before I fished at night
Wading in hunter's obsession,
When, sudden from the stars
The wiped-out dream shone clear,
Struck down my arm.

Awake, I watched myself watching
And being the man
Seeing 'everything as it is,
infinite'.

The clue to all was mine,
I only had to write it down,
But with each step towards a word
It slipped away
Like handcupped water.
Two days stared blank
Until a fragment
Seemed remembered:

Rats running in a bare room,
Tail-furrows in plaster dust.
One turned to look directly, deep,
Took time to groom its whiskers,
Followed the others into a hole.

Two Swifts at Standlake

I caught no trout today,
But saw two swifts
Flickering above the lake,
Intertwining courtly circles.

Line astern four pinions
Stroked high together,
Slow-moving air-treading,
For the gentle mounting,
Mutual fleeting tremble.

Freewheeling out of sight
They left me earthbound,
Reflecting how clumsy
Comical contrived
Our human coupling is.

I caught no trout today,
I didn't care. I saw
Two flickering swifts
In classic conjugation.

Ancestors

Look where their long track
Slants across the fell,
Tacks clear of mire and crag
To lead us to the peak.

Marvel with me
At the improbable climb
Of intake walls, each stone
Heaved in men's hands.

Consider the net
Of quick-set hedges;
Here's hawthorn for possession,
But count the trespass species

Brought on the wind,
Splashed from a blackbird's gut
Number the centuries of trees,
The torn hands of hedgers.

Memorial and more;
There's inheritance in trods,
In dry-stone walls,
In the slow shaping of a quick hedge.

Mowdywarp

'In the name of God, Amen, Aughust vi th 1663, I John
Ralling Elder of Hollings in Kelton, Yeoman, sound in mind
and alerte in bodye and memorye doc make this my will . . .
unto John Ralling my eldest sune one shooting crossbowe
one frame standing in the house, with my part of the plow
irons that is coulter and sock with my part of the yoakes for
plowing . . . unto my sune Johns daughter Frances a Lambe
or half a crowne in moneye . . .'

Sunday morning, wandering by the Cherwell,
Not focusing, and yet aware of
Dubbined toe-caps, clinging water lenses,
The darker green of grass
Round last year's cowclaps, when
A molehill shuddered, humped,
Spilled out newborn volcano.
A mowdywarp was on the move,
Soil-swimming with spade feet
Through tangled roots;

Loam showing a clay-pipe stem,
Bleached, bitten, bone;
Crumbs of mould tumbling
Fresh into light.

The wake of the mowdywarp reaches back
To boyhood fields by the beck
Below ruined Laverock How,
Where the house wept inwardly
For its cold hearth,
Stairs leading to gaps,
The absence of children.
No life but the flutter of a few
Rhode Island Reds through broken windows
Bringing feather warmth, nest-box indignity
To the built-in black oak dresser
Carved 1675, when all my clan

Was there and all around
At Woodfoot, Hunter How, and Hollins.

They speak still in their testaments,
Rise fleshed from their wills,
Come close as I drink
From the freestone trough they chiselled.
They stand again on the hill,
Hear the lark climb at Laverock How.
We eye the land together,
The past heaped
By Mowdywarp, Earth Thrower.
They smile at the old kenning
And at the new.
As I speak their names,
It is their breath that forms
In the morning air.

Rootcutter

Scrap-iron among nettles –
A wheel, the drum it used to turn,
Part of the casing
Lettered 'Gardner's Cutter'.

Jigsaw pieces that assemble
Into frozen-fingered mornings,
Cold clasping mangolds,
Arm-flailing to bring back feeling,
The East wind's knife.
How you had to heave
To start the wheel,
The pull at the guts
As the drum gouged yellow flesh
Into a willow skep.

While stirks stood
Winter prisoners on dung platforms
Bellowing their demands,
Foul-weather terms that we accepted,
Servants of our obligation,
The contract made with beasts we cage,
All a man undertakes
When he leads out the bull.

Grandmother

I sat in silence
At the long scrubbed table
Seeing again the kicking
Of the new-calved cow,
The swollen udder's wince,
That first pail streaked with blood
Here now in the beasemilk pudding.

We ate as in a ceremony
Of which the words were lost
The ritual no longer understood.
No one smacked his lips
Said that he tasted mystery.
Only Grandmother was sure
Of more than frugality,
That the blood was meant to be eaten.

Only Grandmother was certain
That the last sheaf
From the last field of harvest
Had to be offered
By the woman of the house
To the best cow in the byre
On Christmas Day.

Horns turned to our coming,
The glint of wet muzzles
Worn chains wide-open eyes
At midwinter milking.
The chosen one tongue-wrapped her gift,
Rattled the manger for more.
Around us the lift and fall of ribs
Moistness of breath and fresh dung warmth,
Shadows leaping the rafters,
And beyond the swathe of the hurricane lamp
A dark corner by the foddergang.

We did not see the goddess in the corn
Captured double chewed, cast out
To live again in next year's fields.
We did not see in the darkest dark
A woman chained
Her blood anointing seeds.

Only Grandmother glimpsed beyond the byre
The beasemilk's secret power,
Prayer in the sheaf for the sun's return,
An old cry for the earth to quicken.

Sap-Whistle

Smooth-skinned sap-flooded
Hedgerow sycamore was best,
Bigger boys showed that
And where to make a half-moon notch,
How to circle-cut the bark,
Soothe with spit the knock
The repeated knock
Of the back of the knife,
But it was Grandmother's spell,
As if she held a willow wand,
Her doggerel, 'Willy willy wap,
Tip tip tap, take off your black cap',
That compelled the bark
To slide complete,
White thigh revealed.

The rest was paring, trial, craft,
Hollowing an inner space;
Wood wetted in the mouth
To ease the tube in place,
Exact match of nick and notch.
Then a young note piped
From her old breath.

Each year still when red wrinkles
Swell to burst the buds,
When young sap floods I make a whistle
Taste the maple, speak her spell.
I would hand it on but my grandson plays
Half a century from my hedgerow.

Feathers

Each morning fresh feathers on the floor
As if hens had been here secretly
Dust-bathing, scratching around,
Light Sussex, Plymouth Rock,
Rhode Island Red, identified.

Through the fifty-year-old ticking
Of inherited cushions comes
An insistent tapping till
The beak breaches the shell.

Then the duties of grain and water,
The flock half-flying towards me,
Locking at dusk against the fox,
Lifting the slide in the morning
For hen palaver down the gangplank;
The importance of gently carried eggs,

And in due season, each neck pulled
Until the bone broke sudden,
The admired knack of killing –
Though one tough old cock
Had to be chopped with a swatch
On the block by the stick-heap.
It reared headless
Staggered six or seven steps
Spouting its arch of blood –

Aprons of feathers plucked
From warm pimpled flesh,
Fingernails picking out
Ink-laden embryo quills,
The awed mystery of entrails,
The unfinished sequence in the oviduct.

I choose a red cock hackle,
Stroke back the fibres standing proud
With sheen and glint, alive.
I'll tie a fly, there's buoyancy here,
A past that I can hold
To catch a trout tomorrow.

Winter Digging

The feel of wood, worn to my hand,
The heave of the body's lever –
This heavy loam holds more
Than the weight of winter rain.

I carry compost, cover it
Until the tines shine silver
For the buried season's seedbed
That the frost and sun
Will consummate.
Always the land continues.

Blisters, muscle-ache,
A clinging shirt,
Are less than tokens of old toil,
And yet, how close and tight
The fit of earth in fingernails,
The bond with those who bred me.

Hooks in the Ceiling

When the day came
That no one filled the trough,
The pig squealed as if it knew
Why knives were singing on the stone;
Through the afternoon it squealed
As if it smelt the fresh-scrubbed slab;
All night the dogs could not rest
From replying;
Morning squeals fought the ropes
Till the pole-axe fell.

Scalded and shaved, the carcass
Was split through the spine.
All that was good was used.
We feasted on what we had cared for,
And kicked the bladder round the yard.

Through the dark winter,
If we forgot to duck our heads,
A side of bacon's salted thump
Told us again of the weight
Of what hung from the hooks.

Eskdale Dry-Stone Wall

See, here by the holly tree
Above the highest meadow,
This Eskdale dry-stone wall,
A warted lichen-dappled caterpillar
That clasps and humps the how,
Shuffles across the scree's frost litter,
Creeps round the shoulder of the fell,
A line of beauty
Not made to please the eye.

Ever since a glacier cast them wide,
The stones have called to everyone
To put them back together again.
The waller understood
How stones want to bed
Inward leaning on each other,
Through-stones tying them together,
Still in their moment of mutual tension,
Standing for intake, and enclosure won
From forest, or stolen from common.
Many backs ached, segged hands bled
In this labour great as a pyramid
Built for the lord by the dispossessed.

See, here by the holly tree
Where an off-comer's tread
Has broken down old history,
The inner stones are stained
With holly berry red.

Who Needs a Dictionary for That?

Their hands are dancing, more than mime;
Precise positions, Cupped, Compressed,
First Finger, Fist, and One Point Hand
Hold words and syntax in the air.

He draws a story of a monster
Who saves a girl and takes her
To his bed. He is kind, the monster,
He has an electric blanket.

The teacher explains about pylons
And plugs, unties a tangle,
Rewires a circuit till the light
Shines in his emphatic nod.

Her fingers carve like swifts,
Hang still as kestrels.
The fledgling hesitates,
Then flies another word.

He cannot overhear,
Each word has to be shown
Before he shapes it in his hands
To build his slender store.

But look, they hardly watch
The words, they read the face.
How close they come!
Who needs a dictionary for that?

Multiple Handicaps

Neon-light demons
Menace him mute,
Wasting muscles fell him.

We hold him, enfold him
To shuffle and whisper,
Comfort his crying.

They want to ascertain
His academic level.
Can he enumerate demons?

Each day he's dying
While they build their paper
Pyramid about him.

Brahmacharya

'Gandhi's practice of brahmacharya – an old man sleeping
with young girls in order to test his power to abstain – was
slightly absurd. But he was sincere in this, and glad to
discuss it.' (*The Guardian* 6.7.77)

They met on strangely common ground
To discuss their practised
Sleeping with young girls.

The sensual man spoke
Of the bloom on first fruits,
Counted the cores of his conquests.

The holy man told
Of his ecstasy in turning
Away from fleshed desire.

They talked of love,
Making it without creating it,
And vice versa.

Did they consider
The possibility that each of them
Loved only himself?

Hundredth Birthday

If you had your sight
I would send you snaps
Of your great-great nephew
Learning to swim.

If you had your hearing
I would come and talk
About the Ruby Wedding –
Who was there.

If you had your memory
I would ask about ancestors.
Your Grandfather, did he
Remember Waterloo?

If you knew whose cake
You were eating,
If you only knew your name
And where you were,
I could raise my glass,

But that must wait:
I will celebrate the steady tick
Of your longcase clock
When the stranger has gone.

Then I will see you
Come clear of the shade,
I will sing and rejoice
At your funeral.

Grow Potatoes

I am not here to be kind to worms,
But as I dig I cover them with care
To work out their landmarks.

The blackbird is not unkind when he
Makes up his looped moustache
For gaping mouths.

I do not feel unkind to worms when I
Collect them from wet lawns at night
To lure a salmon.

Worms will use me in the end.
They will not be unkind
As they turn me over.

You are not here to be kind to bones.
Don't plant a rose,
Grow potatoes on my grave.